Enough ... 50 years of working out this thing called "life"*

Andrea Gilbertson

Enough ... 50 years of working out this thing called "life"* © 2023 Andrea Gilbertson

Presentation by *BookLeaf Publishing*

Web: www.bookleafpub.com

E-mail: info@bookleafpub.com

ISBN: 9789357442152

First edition 2023

... for all those who have ever felt (or been told they 'are') 'stupid' or 'lazy' or 'fat' or 'misunderstood' ...

... this mini collection is for you ...

.... hopefully you can gain some clarity or awareness or knowledge from some of my musings ....

I Go To The Sea

I go to the sea
when I need some space,
to feel the salt tingle on my face

I go to the sea to clear my head
to breathe in deep
when I'm seeing red

As the cool fresh sea air caresses my tongue
reminding me of beach days
when we were young
running free without a care
the coarse sand sticking everywhere

I take myself there every day,
even if only in my mind,
to stay
true and centred
grounded and calm
the sea working its magic
like a soothing balm

Feeling the sand between my toes
Grounding me
Releasing my woes

The cries of seagulls in the air
Feeling the breeze blowing through my hair
THAT smell of the sea as it fills your nose
the salt dust clinging to your clothes

Picturing the waves as they caress the shore
Hear the anger of Neptunes guttural roar
The taste of watery cocoa from the outdoor pool
Where we'd swim to ease our stress
After a day at school

I swim in the sea
To be at one with the waves
To feel her power
That my soul craves

I swim in the sea to feel alive
Do I dare to take a dive ?
The rush of water over my skin
The gasp as I dare to enter in
I feel my heart pump
The rush of blood
Through every vein
The awakening flood
Every cell tingles from head to toe
The sea with her magical healing flow

I go to the sea
When I need to be
When I need to feel my truest me

Just A Mask

I wasn't a boy
I didn't cause pain
I didn't disrupt again and again

I wasn't 'enough'
naughty or mad
my own internal version of sad

Hidden away for only me
never wanting anyone to see
how every day was such a chore
what really went on behind closed doors ?

What went on behind my mask ?
why didn't anyone ever ask ?
what is wrong ?
are you OK ?
why do you have to live this way ?

shut everyone off and they'll go away
to just get through another day
existing, just, but it's okay

The daily exhaustion
the daily mess
every minute just doing 'my best'

50 years of what was my 'norm'
regretting ever being born
anything to numb the 'pain'
sabotage again and again

You're 'clever' why are you such a fool
it's been like this since infant school
but no-one dared enough to ask

Are you really OK ?

Or is it just a mask ?

You Would Be Pretty

You would be pretty if you weren't so fat ....

Who the **** would say a thing like that ?
A woman who really 'should' have known better
...
If only I had never met her ...

Instead I had to suffer a role as her 'niece' ...
Her constant belittling of me being 'obese' ...

Puffed cheeks
Weak teeth
Fake smile
Dead eyes
Self loathing my 'disgusting' thighs

Lax addiction
Pushing down pain
A daily battle avoiding 'weight gain'
If only I was 'thin' I'd be 'enough'
The facade that I was really 'tough' ...

If only I could turn back time
And tell 'young me' she was sublime
Hence why others tried to dim her light

Making her life a daily fight
Against the demons in her head
Telling herself she'd be better off dead

Hindsight can be a wonderful thing
To give you the power that only healing can
bring

So now my purpose is to share these words
So others can finally really feel heard

Stand up to those who's words cut deep
The bullies left alone to weep

The axe never remembers
The tree never forgets

A life once filled with deep regret
Let it all go
Move forward with pride
Your true beauty radiates from deep inside
Let go of the past
Release the pain
Free yourself all over again

LIVE ... don't EXIST

Your best life's on its way

Make the most of every day

No more hiding

No more fear

You are ENOUGH

This is YOUR year

Environment is Everything

Environment is everything
It's how a flower blooms
It's how you feel,
your energy
when you walk in a room

If you feel you aren't blooming
aren't achieving your potential
you may find that a fresh new start
turns out to be essential

Sometimes the darkness feels like
you've been buried in the earth
but maybe you've been planted
ready for your new 're birth'

So if you're in a dark place
and something isn't right
find your new environment
and turn that dark to light

The Snack

The Snack

Oh why did you just eat that snack?
Did you just feel a need ?
Why did you REALLY eat that snack?
Was it just a moment of 'greed'?

Were you just trying to fill a hole?
That emptiness inside?
You can't quite put your finger on?
The pain you really hide?

Did you just need to find the crunch
That puts anger at bay
The feeling that you need to munch
To just get through today

That mask you wear?
The 'I'm ok'?
The tales you tell yourself each day ...

The 'comfort' you get from that box of chocs
The discomfort you feel putting on your socks
The pain in your knees
As you climb the stairs

Just block it out
Who really cares?

That impulsive decision
Where you had no voice
Why did I just do that?
Did I have a choice?

Things can be different
Now maybe try
To change the meaning of your WHY?

I deserve to be happy
I deserve to fully LIVE
Instead of just existing
This to myself I'll give

There's no time like the present
So from now on I will be
Giving myself the greatest gift
To live the best version of me

ADHD - Time Blindness

Where have the last 5 hours gone?
I had so much to do!
And now the past is just a blur
And I feel guilty too

So now I'll waste another hour 'stuck' in guilt
and shame
Instead of just forgiving myself
I'm not the one to blame
My brain is just a little 'wrong'
Doesn't do what it should do
The front and back don't communicate
The little 'wires' are screwed
So now I'll sit a little more
To wallow and to brood
And then I'll make myself a list
And make myself some food

I must be kinder to myself
I must learn more self care
I'm trying every single day
One day we might get 'there'

Grandma get your thesaurus out

Grandma, get your thesaurus out!
I heard some new words today!
I heard a boy on my walk from school
He said 'my ******* mother is gay'

Grandma, what is this word '*****ng'?
Grandma, what is this word 'gay' ?
She tried her best to shush me
Not one more word I'd say ...

My Grandda's face grew redder
I'd never heard him shout!
Go to your room!
Never use that word again!
Go and wash your dirty mouth out!

Eight years old
Full of dread
What on earth had I just said ?!

My Grandma came and got me
She knew I just loved to learn
My Grandda looked out the window
With a look of grave concern

Where had his 'innocent baby' gone
My mouth no longer pure
He gave me a hug and all was well
No more silence to endure

We got the game of Boggle out
Normality returned
And there, across the dice appeared
THAT word that I'd just learned ...

True

I really was a 'quirky' child
I didn't 'conventionally' 'play'
My 'best friends' were my Grandparents
I saw them every day

Every day I'd learn new 'stuff'
New things we'd bake and cook,
Do crosswords, rhymes and puzzles,
Learning words from my favourite book

The 'family' never understood
Why I chose to spend my days
'Playing' with my grandparents
With our 'weird' fun-filled ways

"You're obsessed by that thesaurus"
It's not 'normal' for a child
Why aren't you like the other kids?
Outdoors running wild

But outdoors they all bullied me
Inside I felt protected
Happy, safe, and full of joy
Loved and not rejected

Years later I would learn those years
Of learning weren't in vain
The words I learnt have helped me
To release my entrenched pain

And now I share my store of words
With those who have never felt 'heard'
Sharing is caring
So this is my way
To share the value of my 'weird play'

Don't let others tell you
What's 'weird' or what is 'wrong'
As long as you are happy
And feel like you 'belong'
Then that is all that matters
Who matters most is YOU
And that's the most important thing
Stay happy, real and true

Dance With Me

Please just come and dance with me
Don't fear what others think!
I just want you to dance with me
Why do you need another drink?

Just let me have another shot
Before I hit the floor
Just one more shot to numb the 'fear'
I've felt this all before

I so want to be fearless
Dancing so carefree
Just like I do when in my room
When there is only me

Letting my body feel the flow
Spinning fast, waving slow
Arms raised swooshing through the air
All alone, no one there
To judge or shame or criticise
Making me feel watched by a thousand eyes

Thank you for teaching me not to think
I need the 'confidence' from a drink
If anyone judges
The issue is theirs
As I wildly dance
No-one stares

Thanks to you for teaching me
To be who I was never 'allowed' to be
So judged and shamed
Controlled and 'scared'
Of what 'others' thought
That others 'cared'

The power of dancing wild and free
Happiness washing over me
The confidence to just not care
What others think when I am there
In a world of my own
In the middle of the floor
Just feeling the vibe
Surrounded by my 'tribe'
All of us with just one goal
To feel that music in our soul

Why did I allow what others said
To stop me dancing,
Full of dread
'What would 'others' think ?'
'What would 'others' say ?'

Now I don't care

And that's ok

My final final final straw

I know I've said it all before
But today really was my 'final straw'
The shame I felt right to my core
When I couldn't get up off the floor

Without the help of a nearby seat
To get myself up on my feet
Enough I thought
This is not OK
Existing like this every day

Choosing life based on whether my ass fits
Conscious wherever I have to sit
If a chair is strong enough to 'take the strain'
Aware of the 'spread' when I sit on a train
Hoping nobody sits next to me
When they do, apologising profusely
'Sorry I'm taking up half of your seat'
(I want this journey to end so I can go home and
eat …
away the humiliation, guilt and shame)
'I'm never getting back on a train'
Till the next time and the same story all over
again ….

The theatre seat as it makes a creak
I'm now conscious of the 'spread'
I cough to hide the 'eeeking sound'
Wish I could afford 2 seats instead
At least that would ease my burden that
I'm 'taking up too much room'
My favourite hobby blighted
By my inner voice of doom

The dread of flying when you have to say
'please can I have an extension belt today ?'

I know there is an 'easier' way to stop this 'fest
of shame'
I need to just accept myself
I wasn't the one to blame
But now I am an adult
No-one can do 'this' but me
So now the time has come for my accountability

So today I made the first step
To where I want to be
And step by step
Day by day
I'll get back to my best 'me'

Oh kids they are resilient

Oh kids they are resilient
What happens if they're not ?
What if they are sensitive
And can't handle a lot ?

What if they just aren't 'like you'
What if they aren't 'tough'
What if the words you say to them
Make them feel not 'enough'

Not everyone is made the same
The nurture vs nature 'game'

What if they must hide their pain
Too fearful to speak out
How peoples actions hurt them
But they're too afraid to shout

So then they go for decades
Feeling so unheard
The pain it eats away at them
They must not say a word

They must obey
They must do well
Some secrets they must 'never tell'

Then people wonder why they rebel
When they can take no more
If only they'd been listened to
Years and years before

But now its too late for that child
And everyone wonders why
'But they were always happy'
'I never once saw them cry'

'The life and soul of the party'
'Made everybody laugh'

Everyone except for them

The child who didn't laugh last …

The ADHD Menopausal Head

Somedays I just feel 'lazy'
Somedays I just feel 'flat'
My brains a little 'hazy'
Why did I just do that ?

Why does my head lose track of time
For hours and hours on end
Why can't I be efficient
Like that 'Mary Poppins' friend

But girl you're just 'bone idle'
But girl you are just 'fat'
But girl you are just 'lazy'
You must know all of that ?

But nope I'm not bone idle
Lazy or 'just fat'
My brain is 'just dysfunctional'
And now that I know that

I can't control my impulses
Dopamine's my best mate
Everything is double hard
Because my brain's a state

5 decades it took to work it out
I fell through 'all the nets'
Apparently I was 'masking'
A life filled with regrets

A life of 'what if's', 'could have beens'
And what I achieved 'before'
A life that I now realise
I was potentially worth so much more

The life before the menopause
When I was just able to cope
These hormones they've now thrown me off
And today I've just lost hope
So I'll try again tomorrow
Tomorrow I'll 'succeed'
Tomorrow I'll do 'better'
Tomorrow I'll believe
That one day I'll be 'me' again
The one who can get by
The one who's normal's not normal
The one who wishes she'd asked why?

The one who gets in bed at night proud of what
I've achieved
Not this current version who just feels so
aggrieved

The one who thinks this 'normal' is how she
must go on
But that is just the way it is
It's what she's always done

And one day I will realise just how much
strength I've had
To just get through yet another day with a brain
that is just 'bad'

Thank You

To all those friends who got me through
Thank you for just being you
Thank you for just being there
Thank you for letting me know you care

Thank you for being a piece of the jigsaw that
fixed my broken heart
Thank you whether you've just arrived or been
here from the start

Thank you for being part of my healing
No matter how big or small
You helped me get back on my feet
After my biggest fall
No matter how big or small your part
Even if it was just one call
That may have been a day when I was gonna
end it all

The most precious thing in life you can give
To someone is your time
Thank you for sharing yours with me
You really are sublime

Thank you for being part of my tribe
You're the reason why I'm still alive
Thank you for being part of my crew

Thank you for being you

The Catharsis in a Pen

A pen can be your most powerful tool
To heal from deep inside
The more you write
The more you release
To reveal all that you hide

The more you write
The more you clear the 'stuff' that's in your
head
Healing is a journey
Things not better left unsaid

Release the words
Release the pain
Allow the ink to flow
Feel it in your body as you're ready to let go

Strip those layers all away
The more that you reveal
Reveals the space for energy
The energy to heal

If you can't find the words to say
Just write anything every day

One day you will work it out, consistency is key

Till one day you will realise ….

You'll realise you're free

An Ode to Progress not Perfection

.... this is progress ....

An ode to ADHD

.... deadlines 0 ....

.... ADHD 1 ....

An ode to Procrastination

.... deadlines 0 ....

.... Procrastination 1 ....

ADHD in a nutshell

I missed my deadline ....

I did finish 14 poems though ! ....

Go Me !!! ....

If you know you know !!!! .....

www.ingramcontent.com/pod-product-compliance
Lightning Source LLC
LaVergne TN
LVHW010934200726

843509LV00013B/2213